CCSS **Genre** Biography

W9-AKV-614

? Essential Question
How can one person make a difference?

Jacob Riis
Champion of the Poor

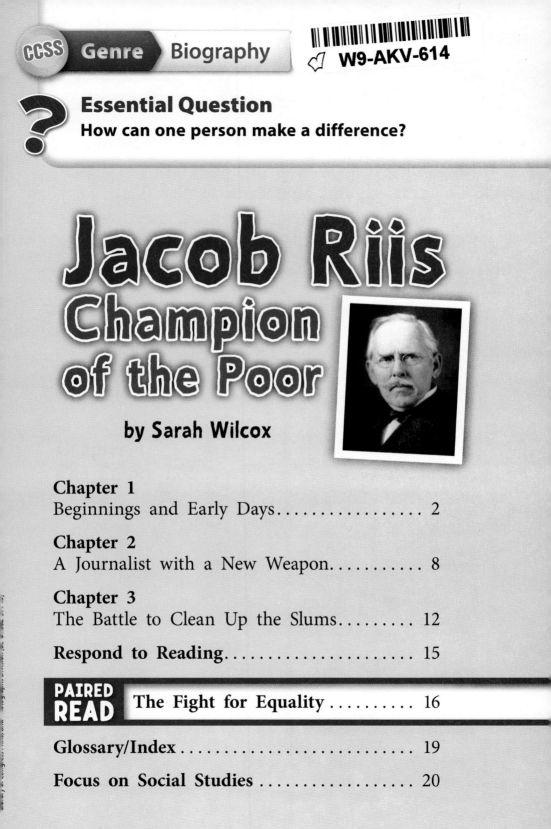

by Sarah Wilcox

In 1870, Jacob Riis **immigrated** to the United States. He traveled from Denmark to New York. At the time, many immigrants came to New York. They were looking for a better life. Instead, they lived in **slums**. The slums were dark, dirty, and overcrowded places. Diseases spread easily. Some people even died.

Riis experienced the life of an immigrant. He wanted people to understand how hard life was for new immigrants.

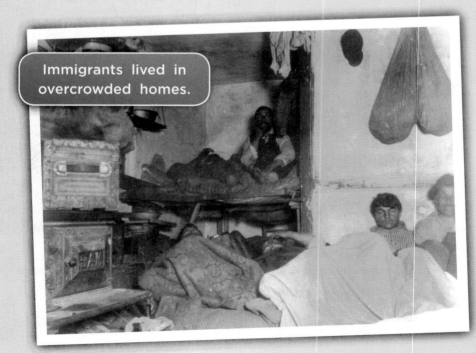

Immigrants lived in overcrowded homes.

Riis became a journalist. He wrote stories about immigrants. Riis used photography to tell the stories. Riis's photographs <u>were a window into</u> the lives of the people who lived in the slums. He wanted to make life better for the poor.

In Other Words let people see. En español, *were a window into* quiere decir *permitieron ver como era*.

Thousands of children lived in slums in New York City.

Jacob Riis was born in 1849 in Ribe, Denmark. He learned English in school and trained to become a carpenter.

Riis met a young woman named Elisabeth Nielsen. He wanted to marry Elisabeth, but her stepfather was against the marriage. Riis could not find work, so he immigrated to the United States. He was 21 years old. Riis thought there were better opportunities in the United States. He planned to get a job and make money, then return to Denmark to marry Elisabeth.

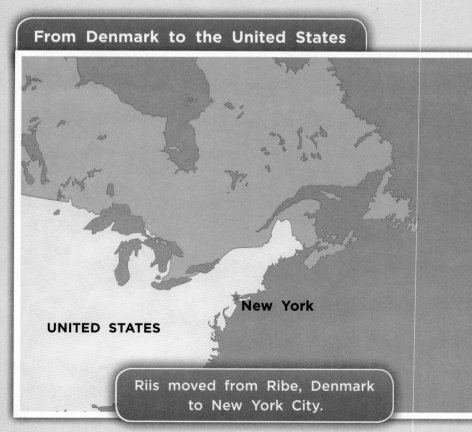

From Denmark to the United States

New York

UNITED STATES

Riis moved from Ribe, Denmark to New York City.

When Riis arrived in New York City in 1870, he worked many jobs. He also worked as a carpenter, miner, and farmhand. He worked on the railroad and wrote stories for magazines.

Sometimes Riis was paid well. Other times, he was mistreated by his employers. They paid him less than they had promised. Sometimes Riis did not have enough money for food or a place to sleep.

After three years, Riis was still poor. Would he be able to fulfill his dream to marry Elisabeth?

DENMARK

Ribe

ATLANTIC OCEAN

It was difficult for immigrants to find jobs. They were not qualified for jobs that paid well. They lived in overcrowded and dirty apartment buildings, called **tenements,** in slums.

Landlords crowded people into tenements. Then they could collect as much rent as possible. As many as 15 people lived in one room.

Many rooms in the tenements were underground. There was no light or fresh air. People had to share the bathrooms.

Immigrants lived in tenements like this one.

MASS IMMIGRATION

Millions of people people immigrated to the United States between 1847 and 1930. Many immigrants came from countries in Europe, such as Ireland, Italy, and Germany.

Some immigrants lived under bridges or in sheds. Riis wrote about these places: "No pig would have been content to live in such a place."

Five Points was a poor neighborhood in New York City. Most people in Five Points lived in tenements and sheds. Many people didn't have jobs. Many children did not go to school. They did not have a place to play. Riis hated to see people live unhappily.

STOP AND CHECK

What was life like for immigrants in New York?

sheds

Many people in the Five Points slum lived in sheds.

Bettmann/CORBIS

In 1873, Riis began to work as a reporter for the New York News Association. Riis wrote about injustice and the terrible living conditions of poor people. Riis pointed out that New York City had more than one million people who were <u>living</u> in **poverty**. Riis later wrote in his book *How the Other Half Lives*, "These sights [of poverty] gripped my heart. I must tell of them or burst."

Now that Riis had a job, he returned to Denmark to marry Elisabeth. Then they returned to the United States together.

Jacob's wife Elisabeth poses with their first child, Edward.

Language Detective	<u>Living</u> is the main verb. What is the helping verb?

Back in New York City, Riis worked as a police reporter for the *New York Tribune* from 1877 to 1888. The job gave Riis opportunities to write stories about living in the slums.

Riis believed that education and better living conditions would change the lives of poor people. He knew he had to convince people that his stories about poverty were true.

In 1887, Riis read about a way to take photographs in the dark. It was called flash photography. The photographer used a special powder to make a bright light.

Before 1887, it wasn't possible to take photographs in dark places. The slums were full of dark places, so photographs could not show what the slums looked like. Riis realized that he could use flash photography to take photographs of the dark places in the slums.

Riis was one of the first journalists to use flash photography to tell his stories.

It was dangerous to use flash photography. Riis needed people to help him light the powder for the flash. The powder could be unsafe to use. Once, the flash powder exploded in his face. Fortunately, Riis was wearing glasses, and his eyes were not harmed.

STOP AND CHECK

How did flash photography help Jacob Riis?

Library of Congress, Prints & Photographs Division [LC-USZ62-39057]

Riis used flash photography to take photos of children sleeping on the streets in New York City.

HOW TO TAKE A PHOTOGRAPH WITH FLASH POWDER

1. First, the photographer set up the camera on a tripod.

2. Then, the photographer ground the two flash powders separately.

3. Next, the photographer mixed the powders together.

4. Then, the photographer lit a match and threw it on the flash powder. He had to be careful not to get too close!

5. Finally, the photographer took a picture when the flash was shining.

Sometimes the photographer didn't grind the powders separately before mixing them. This could cause an explosion or a fire.

flash

This photo shows a photographer in 1884 using magnesium to create a flash. Flash powder worked in a similar way.

Riis's photographs of the slums <u>were</u> printed with his stories in newspapers. The photographs shocked the readers. Riis showed his photographs during lectures he gave at public meetings. He talked about the need to improve life in the slums.

In 1890, Riis published a book called *How the Other Half Lives*. The book described what Riis had seen and experienced in the slums of New York.

Riis's book *How the Other Half Lives* was very popular.

Language Detective	<u>Were</u> is the helping verb. What is the main verb?

newspaper

board

Riis took this photo of a men's lodging room in 1892. The men slept on boards on the floor or on newspapers.

The New York police commissioner, Theodore Roosevelt, read Riis's book. Roosevelt provided encouragement to Riis. They became good friends. Roosevelt later became President of the United States.

How the Other Half Lives inspired city officials to improve living conditions of the poor. They worked to clean up the Five Points slum.

It took 14 years to tear down the Five Points slum. Riis's work helped to improve life for many people in New York City.

Riis wrote more books and gave lectures. He continued to speak out for the poor.

Jacob Riis died in 1914. New York City named a park after him. There is also a school and a playground named in his memory.

STOP AND CHECK

How did Riis help the poor?

ocean

beach

People enjoy the beach at Jacob Riis Park.

THE LIFE OF JACOB RIIS

1849: Riis is born in Ribe, Denmark.

1870: Riis immigrates to the United States.

1876: Riis marries Elisabeth Nielsen.

1877: Riis begins working as a newspaper reporter.

1888: Riis first uses flash photography.

1890: Riis's book *How the Other Half Lives* is published.

1914: Riis dies.

Respond to Reading

Summarize

Use important details to summarize how Jacob Riis helped the poor. Your graphic organizer may help you.

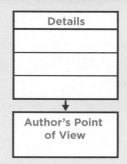

Text Evidence

1. What kind of informational text is *Jacob Riis: Champion of the Poor*? What text features tell you that? GENRE

2. What does the author think of living conditions in the slums? Use details from the text to figure out the author's point of view. AUTHOR'S POINT OF VIEW

3. Find a synonym for the word *unsafe* on page 10. What is an antonym for *unsafe*? SYNONYMS AND ANTONYMS

4. Does the author think that Jacob Riis made a difference to the people living in slums? Write about the author's point of view. Use evidence from the text. WRITE ABOUT READING

Compare Texts

Read about how a young girl made a difference in her community.

The Fight for Equality

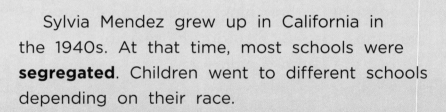

Sylvia Mendez grew up in California in the 1940s. At that time, most schools were **segregated**. Children went to different schools depending on their race.

Access Denied

When Sylvia was eight years old, her parents tried to register her at the local school. They learned that the school was only for white children. Sylvia's parents were Mexican and Puerto Rican. The school for non-white children was far away. It was in an old building. The school for white children was in a new building.

Martin H. Simon/CORBIS

Victory in California

Sylvia's parents thought it was unfair that Sylvia was being treated differently because of her race.

Her parents and the local community protested segregation in schools. They sued the school district and won. During the trial, Sylvia had to speak in front of the judge. She had to prove that she could speak English.

In 1947, California became the first state to end segregation in schools. Soon people in other states protested, too. They held boycotts. By 1969, the protests had helped <u>bring about</u> the end of segregation in schools. Children no longer had to go to different schools because of their race.

In Other Words make happen. En español, *bring about* quiere decir *causar*.

People are protesting against segregation in schools in St. Louis, Missouri, in 1963.

Life After School

Sylvia went to the school that had been only for white children. Sometimes students teased her, but she did not give up. She studied hard and became a nurse.

Today, Sylvia Mendez speaks at schools and encourages students to study. She teaches them about the importance of getting a good education.

In 2011, Sylvia received the Presidential Medal of Freedom. She received the medal for the work she has done for **civil rights** in education.

President Barack Obama presents Sylvia with her medal.

Martin H. Simon/CORBIS

Make Connections

How did Sylvia Mendez make a difference? **ESSENTIAL QUESTION**

Jacob Riis and Sylvia Mendez both made a difference in their communities. How are they similar? How are they different? **TEXT TO TEXT**

Glossary

civil rights the rights everyone has *(page 18)*

immigrated moved from their home country to a new country *(page 2)*

poverty the state of being poor *(page 8)*

segregated separated by race *(page 16)*

slums the run-down areas of a city, inhabited by poor people *(page 2)*

tenements buildings that have many rented rooms or apartments, which are often in bad condition *(page 6)*

Index

Focus on
Social Studies

Purpose To show how kids can make a difference in their communities

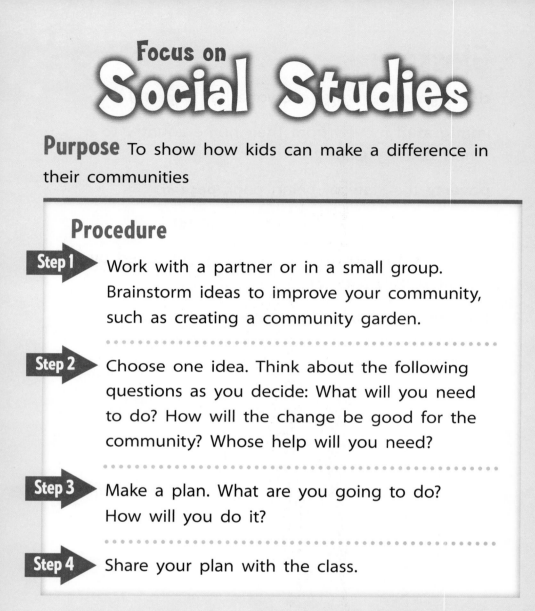

Procedure

Step 1 Work with a partner or in a small group. Brainstorm ideas to improve your community, such as creating a community garden.

Step 2 Choose one idea. Think about the following questions as you decide: What will you need to do? How will the change be good for the community? Whose help will you need?

Step 3 Make a plan. What are you going to do? How will you do it?

Step 4 Share your plan with the class.